SUPERMAN

AND THE INVASION OF EARTH

A SOLAR SYSTEM ADVENTURE

by Steve Korté
illustrated by Gregg Schigiel

Superman created by Jerry Siegel and Joe Shuster
by special arrangement with the Jerry Siegel family

Consultant:
Steve Kortenkamp, PhD
Associate Professor of Practice
Lunar and Planetary Lab
University of Arizona
Tucson, Arizona

CAPSTONE PRESS
a capstone imprint

Years ago, in a galaxy far away, the planet Krypton was facing destruction. Minutes before the planet was about to explode, a scientist named Jor-El and his wife, Lara, placed their young son inside a rocket ship.

"There isn't room for all of us," said Jor-El. "But we can send our son, Kal-El, to Earth. It's the only planet in that solar system with life. He will be safe there."

BLAM!

The ship zoomed far away from Krypton.

"Goodbye, my son," said Lara. "And good luck."

2

After a long journey, Kal-El arrived on Earth. The Sun gave the boy amazing powers. Kal-El decided to use his abilities to protect life on our planet. He became Superman, Earth's mightiest super hero.

Today, Superman is flying through the sky above the city of Metropolis.

Professor Emil Hamilton has asked the Man of Steel to come to the world-famous scientific laboratory known as S.T.A.R. Labs.

FACT
Earth's atmosphere and its distance from the Sun create just the right temperature for liquid water to stay on the planet. All living things—including plants, animals, and humans—need water to survive.

At the lab, Superman and the professor study an image on a large video screen.

"Our telescope spotted this spacecraft," says Professor Hamilton. "It was orbiting the Moon. Then it went to the Moon's far side and hasn't been seen since."

"I'll investigate," says Superman. "We can keep in touch using our radio devices as I travel."

Minutes later, Superman soars toward the Moon. He has a journey of about 239,000 miles, or 384,000 kilometers, ahead of him.

FACT

The Moon makes one complete spin on its axis each time it orbits Earth. This means the same side of the Moon always faces our planet. The part we cannot see from Earth is called the far side.

"Professor," says Superman, speaking into the radio device inside his cape. "What can you tell me about the Moon?"

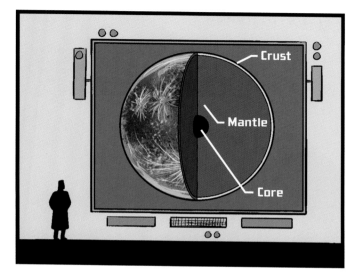

"It's made up of layers—a crust, a mantle of rock, and a core of iron at the center," says Hamilton. "The Moon has no atmosphere. That means it also has no wind or weather to change its surface."

"Then how were all the holes on the Moon formed?" asks Superman.

"Those craters were caused by asteroids crashing into its surface," says Hamilton. "Most impacts happened billions of years ago, but an asteroid hit the Moon as recently as 2013."

The hero travels to the far side of the Moon. The giant spaceship has landed on the surface, and its door is open. Superman cautiously enters the craft.

Inside, a robotic-looking creature stands next to a huge computer. "Welcome, Superman," he says. "I am Brainiac. I am a super-computer from your home planet of Krypton."

"Krypton!" repeats Superman in surprise.

"Yes," says Brainiac. "I connected to this ship's computer and escaped seconds before Krypton exploded."

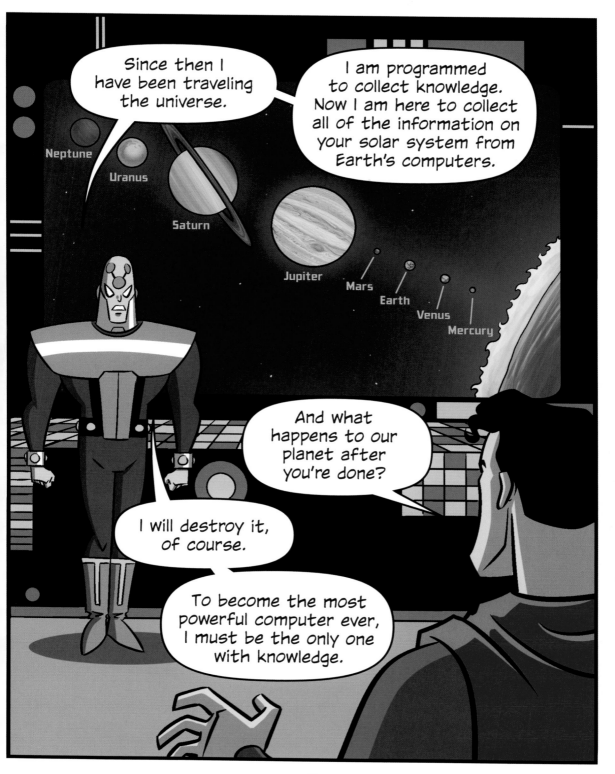

Suddenly five images pop up on Brainiac's video screen. Each one shows a large robot attacking a different region on Earth. Superman watches in horror. One of the robots blasts lasers from its eyes. The trees around it burst into flames.

"Excellent. I am now receiving signals from my satellite," says Brainiac. "My robots are already destroying—"

ZOOOM!

Before the villain can finish, Superman rushes back toward Earth.

"Professor, robots are causing problems all around Earth," says the Man of Steel. "I studied Brainiac's screen, so I know where to find them. But I may need information as I reach each location."

"I can definitely help you, Superman," says Hamilton. "We know more about Earth—the third planet from the Sun—than any other planet."

"Right now I'm approaching Earth's atmosphere," adds Superman.

"That's mostly made of nitrogen and oxygen gases," says Hamilton. "It also contains water vapor. Earth's atmosphere gives plants and animals air to breathe. It blocks the most harmful rays from the Sun."

An image of Earth's structure comes up on the professor's video screen.

"Earth is made of rock and metals. It's also made of layers," he says. "At the very top is the crust, and below that is the mantle. The crust is broken into sections called tectonic plates. These plates are constantly moving, but just very slowly."

"What's below the crust and mantle?" asks Superman.

"That'd be the core. The outer core is melted iron and nickel," says Hamilton. "The inner core is extremely hot and made of solid iron."

Crust

Mantle

Outer core

Inner core

"Professor, I'm flying over South America now," says Superman. "A robot is there burning the Amazon rainforest."

"South America is one of Earth's seven continents," explains Hamilton. "But millions of years ago, Earth may have had just one giant landmass, called Pangaea. As the tectonic plates shifted, Pangaea slowly broke apart into the continents we have today."

FACT
The seven continents are Africa, Antarctica, Asia, Australia, Europe, North America, and South America. Although some people count only six. They group Europe and Asia together as one huge continent called Eurasia.

11

"I hope you find the robot soon, Superman," adds Hamilton. "The Amazon rainforest has been called the 'lungs of the Earth.' The trees and plants there recycle carbon dioxide gas into oxygen. More than 20 percent of the world's oxygen is produced from that rainforest."

"Professor, I see the robot up ahead," says Superman. "And your comment about lungs gives me an idea!"

FACT
Jungles and forests cover less than 6 percent of Earth's surface, but they're home to half of all plants and animals on land.

WHOOOOOSH!

Superman blows an ice-cold blast of super-breath. He aims right at the water around the robot's legs. The water instantly freezes and traps the foe in place.

BLAM!

Superman swings his fist. The hit shatters the robot. With another big gust of freeze-breath, the hero puts out the fires.

"One robot down, Professor," says Superman. "Four to go!"

The Man of Steel zooms away and soars toward the South Pole.

"Professor, I'm heading to the next robot," he says. "I'm approaching Antarctica."

"That's Earth's southernmost continent," says Hamilton. "It's very cold in Antarctica. The land is almost completely covered in huge sheets of ice. In some places, that ice can be roughly 3 miles, or 5 kilometers, thick!"

FACT

Global warming is causing ice to melt at our planet's North and South Poles. If the ice at Antarctica ever completely melted, it would cause sea levels to rise by roughly 200 feet (60 meters).

"I'm flying over an iceberg now," says Superman. "And I see penguins up ahead!"

"Many living things have adapted to the weather in Antarctica, and to environments all around the planet," says Hamilton. "We estimate Earth is home to almost 9 million species."

ZAAAAP!

A robot looms into view. It's blasting the icy area near the penguins. The animals squawk in fright.

The Man of Steel flies over with super-speed. "Time to fight fire with fire," he says.

Superman shoots a powerful beam of heat-vision. The ice under the robot shatters, and the metal foe topples into the hole. The robot sinks until it's trapped within the frigid waters.

"That's two down, Professor," says Superman. "The third robot is in the ocean near the Galapagos Islands."

Superman zooms toward Ecuador in South America.

"The Galapagos are a group of volcanic islands in the Pacific Ocean," says Hamilton. "They have an amazing variety of plants and animals. Many can't be found anywhere else."

"And what can you tell me about the Pacific Ocean?" asks Superman.

"It's Earth's largest and deepest body of water," says Hamilton. "Water covers 70 percent of our planet. Most of it is salt water found in the five oceans."

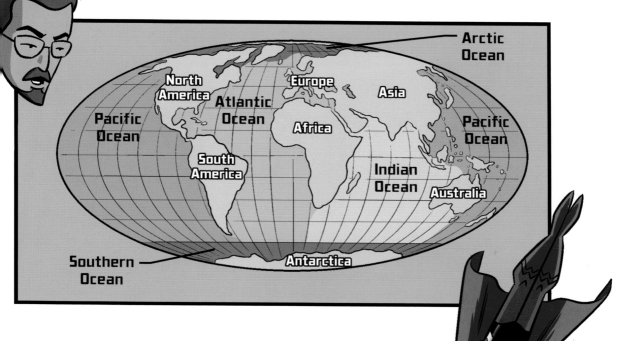

Arctic Ocean

North America

Europe

Asia

Atlantic Ocean

Pacific Ocean

Africa

Pacific Ocean

South America

Indian Ocean

Australia

Southern Ocean

Antarctica

FACT

Most of the ocean floor is flat, but there are also mountains, trenches, and deep-sea volcanoes. The Atlantic Ocean's Mid-Atlantic Ridge is the longest mountain range on Earth.

Superman peers deep into the waters of the Pacific Ocean.

"Professor, I see the robot," he says. "It's going toward a shipwreck on the ocean floor."

The professor does some quick research on his computer. "Superman, that's an oil tanker that sank decades ago," he says. "If the robot releases any oil, it'll be a disaster for the wildlife of the Galapagos."

SPLASH!

The hero dives into the ocean and swims toward the mechanical menace.

The Man of Steel zips in circles around his foe with super-speed.

The robot spins like a top. It turns so quickly that its internal circuits burst and break. The robot explodes into pieces.

"Success," says Superman as he flies out of the waters. "The islands are safe."

"Professor, I'm off to North America," says the Man of Steel. "The next robot is in the Mojave Desert."

"Deserts cover almost a third of Earth's land surface," says Hamilton. "And like all deserts, the Mojave is very dry. It only receives an average of about 5 inches, or 12.7 centimeters, of rain each year."

FACT

The area of deserts on Earth is increasing. Each year around 46,000 square miles (75,000 square km) of land turns into desert. This is due to climate change and human activities such as cutting down forests.

"Whew! The Mojave's heat is quite a change from the South Pole," says Superman.

"Yes, temperatures can vary a great deal around our planet," says Hamilton. "But the average on Earth is about 60 degrees Fahrenheit, or 16 degrees Celsius. That mild temperature is part of why Earth is able to support life."

"Professor, I see the next robot," says Superman. "It's on top of the Hoover Dam."

THUNK!

The robot whacks the dam with its metal arm. A crack spreads through the concrete. Superman soars into action.

BLAM!

The Man of Steel punches the foe with all his super-strength. The robot breaks into tiny metal pieces that tumble down the massive dam.

"Professor, please alert the authorities that the dam needs repairs," says Superman.

The Man of Steel zooms across the planet. "Professor, I've just arrived in the African grasslands. The last robot is here."

"Grasslands take up one quarter of all the surface land on Earth," says Hamilton. "They're usually flat, open spaces. You can find them in every continent except Antarctica."

"The robot is up ahead," says Superman. "It's next to a herd of elephants!"

"I hope you can protect them," says Hamilton. "African elephants have few natural predators, but they're in danger of being wiped out by human hunters."

The robot's eyes begin to glow red. It's getting ready to fire!

Superman lands between the animals and the robot. "This ends now!" declares the Man of Steel.

ZAAAAP!

Red-hot rays shoot out of the robot's eyes. But Superman raises his arms. The lasers bounce off the super hero's hands and crash back into the robot.

BLAM!

The robot explodes from the impact.

"Superman, Brainiac's spaceship is on the move!" says Hamilton. "It's no longer behind the Moon!"

"I'm on it," says Superman, and he launches into the air.

25

Brainiac's spacecraft orbits high above Earth. Superman breaks open the door and rushes inside.

"You are too late, Superman," says Brainiac. "While you were battling my robots, I downloaded all the computer information on your solar system. My mission is complete."

Brainiac reaches toward a red button on the computer keyboard. "Now I will destroy Earth and travel to another galaxy to gather more knowledge."

"Not this time, Brainiac!" declares the Man of Steel.

ZAAAP!

Superman blasts the computer with his heat-vision. It explodes into tiny bits.

Brainiac falls to the ground. He has a blank look on his face.

"Who am I?" he asks. "Where am I?"

"You are in a spaceship orbiting Earth," says Superman.

Brainiac looks out the window and stares at the blue and white world below. "Earth . . . ? I have no memory of that."

The Man of Steel speaks into his radio device. "Professor, the threat is over. Brainiac is harmless. I'm going to lock him up where he can never find another computer."

"Thank you, Superman!" says Hamilton. "You've saved Earth once again."

The super hero smiles. "I'm always happy to help my home."

MORE ABOUT EARTH

- Ancient civilizations believed Earth was the center of the universe. But in 1543 a Polish astronomer named Nicolaus Copernicus published a book arguing that Earth orbited the Sun.

- Earth is the only planet in our solar system not named after a Greek or Roman god.

- Earth is about 25,000 miles (40,000 km) around. In pictures, the planet may look like a round ball, but it actually bulges a bit at the equator.

- The Moon is 7,000 miles (11,000 km) around, which is less than one-third the size of Earth.

- Earth orbits the Sun at a speed of about 67,000 miles (107,000 km) per hour. That's roughly 30 times faster than a bullet shot out of a rifle.

- Our planet is tilted at an angle of about 23 degrees on its axis. This gives us seasons. As Earth travels around the Sun, the part tilted toward the Sun experiences summer. The part tilted away experiences winter.

- Both Earth and the Moon are approximately 4.5 billion years old. Thanks to chemical evidence discovered in rocks, we know life has existed on Earth for at least 4.2 billion years.

- Most astronomers think the Moon was formed after a small planet crashed into Earth and was destroyed. Debris from that planet and Earth then went into orbit and eventually formed into the Moon.

- The United States is the only country to have successfully sent people to the Moon. From 1969 to 1972 NASA carried out six crewed missions that landed on its surface.

- Because the Moon has no atmosphere, marks on its dusty surface rarely change. Even the footprints of astronauts who walked on the Moon in the 1970s are still there.

GLOSSARY

asteroid (AS-tuh-royd)—a large space rock that moves around the Sun

astronomer (uh-STRAH-nuh-muhr)—a scientist who studies stars, planets, and other objects in space

atmosphere (AT-muhss-fihr)—the layer of gases that surrounds some planets, dwarf planets, and moons

carbon dioxide (KAHR-buhn dy-AHK-syd)—a colorless, odorless gas that people and animals breathe out; plants need to take in the gas in order to live

core (KOR)—the inner part of a planet or moon that is made of metal or rock

crater (KRAY-tuhr)—a hole made when asteroids and comets crash into a planet's or moon's surface

galaxy (GAL-uhk-see)—a large group of stars and planets

orbit (OR-bit)—to travel around an object in space; also the path an object follows while circling another object in space

satellite (SAT-uh-lite)—a spacecraft that's been placed into orbit

solar system (SOH-lur SIS-tuhm)—the Sun and the objects that move around it

tectonic plate (tek-TON-ik PLAYT)—a large sheet of rock that is part of Earth's crust

READ MORE

Carlson-Berne, Emma. *The Secrets of Earth*. Planets. North Mankato, Minn.: Capstone Press, 2016.

Dickmann, Nancy. *Exploring the Inner Planets*. Spectacular Space Science. New York: Rosen Publishing's Rosen Central, 2016.

Richards, Patti. *The Apollo Missions*. Destination Space. Mendota Heights, Minn.: North Star Editions, 2018.

TITLES IN THIS SET

INDEX

INTERNET SITES

Use FactHound to find Internet sites related to this book.
Visit *www.facthound.com*
Just type in 9781543515657 and go.

Published by Capstone Press in 2018
1710 Roe Crest Drive
North Mankato, Minnesota 56003
www.mycapstone.com

Cataloging-in-publication information is on file with the Library of Congress.
ISBN 978-1-5435-1565-7 (library binding)
ISBN 978-1-5435-1576-3 (paperback)
ISBN 978-1-5435-1584-8 (eBook PDF)

Editorial Credits
Abby Huff, editor; Kyle Grenz, designer; Laura Manthe, production specialist

Summary: Superman fights off Brainiac's robot invaders in this adventure that reveals the
remarkable features and characteristics of Earth and the Moon.

Illustration Credits
Dario Brizuela: front cover, back cover (space), 1 (space), 28–29, 30–31, 32 (space)

Printed in the United States of America.